MARGARET WISE BROWN

The Diggers

ILLUSTRATED BY DANIEL KIRK

Hyperion Books for Children

NEW YORK

For information address Hyperion Books for Children,
114 Fifth Avenue, New York, New York 10011.

FIRST EDITION

1   3   5   7   9   10   8   6   4   2

Library of Congress Cataloging-in-Publication Data

Brown, Margaret Wise.
The diggers/Margaret Wise Brown;
illustrated by Daniel Kirk — 1st ed.
p.   cm.
Summary: Verses describe the holes that a mole, dog, worm, and rabbit dig,
but none can compare with the work of a man and his steam shovel.
ISBN 0-7868-0006-2 (trade) —
ISBN 0-7868-2001-2 (lib. bdg.)
1. Children's poetry, American.   2. Excavation — Juvenile poetry.
3. Holes — Juvenile poetry.
[1. Steam shovels — Poetry.   2. Holes — Poetry.   3. American poetry.]
I. Kirk, Daniel, ill.   II. Title.
PS3503.R82184D54 1995
811'.52 — dc20
94-7995
CIP
AC

The artwork for each picture is prepared using oil paint on canvas.
This book is set in 18-point Memphis Medium Condensed.

Designed by Julia Gorton

To my sons, Raleigh and Russell
— D. K.

Dig Dig Dig
A mole was digging a hole.

Dig Dig Dig Dig
A dog was digging a hole
under a stone
to bury a bone.

Dig Dig Dig Dig
A worm was digging a hole.
He swallowed the ground
as he wiggled around
and ate his way
toward home.

Dig Dig Dig Dig
A rabbit was digging a hole
next to a mouse
who was digging a house
in a little warm hole in the ground.

Dig Dig Dig Dig
A pirate was digging a hole,
a hole in the sand
to bury his gold
and the   diamonds and rubies he stole.

Dig Dig Dig Dig
In the city
a man was digging a hole.
Monday he dug,
and Tuesday he dug,
Wednesday, Thursday,
and Friday he dug,
and Saturday he dug until

he said, "I feel like a mouse or a mole.
This hole is too little.
This hole must get bigger
and bigger and bigger,
as big as a giant could dig
if he were a digger."

And then came the big digger
made by a man
to dig deeper and deeper—
to crunch up stones
and dinosaur bones
and cavemen's homes
and buried gnomes.

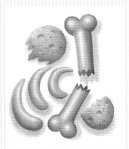

Dig Dig Dig Dig
Down the dead-end street
the steam shovel dug its way.
Day after day after day after day,
it dug
until the whole city street was dug away.

Its great jaws crunched full of dirt and rocks.
Its great arms lifted, paused, and swung
the world it had dug up
and put it somewhere else in the world.

And a great big hole ran under the city
and under a river
and into the bright green country.

A man put a train in the hole,
and the train ran through the hole,
under the street, under the city,
under the river until

it popped out of the hole into the bright green country.

It went past ducks and geese
and donkeys and cows
and sheep and fields of galloping horses
until it came to a mountain
and couldn't get through
and couldn't get over and
couldn't get around so it had to stop.
But not forever—

for down the track came another train
with another man
and tanks of oil
and gasoline.
And there on the last car
rode the great digger, the steam shovel.

Under the mountain it dug away
day after day after day after day
until with one last bite it came to daylight
on the other side of the mountain.

And soon the train came through the mountain
and onto the great green plain.
And on went the train,
on and on down its long steel track,
and the smoke trailed back.

"That was easy," said the steam shovel.
"I'll dig a hole to China someday."